"We've almost forgotten to sing the sun down", says Jeffrey Johnson. He does not, however, forget. In his poems, sun crosses the horizon into night, a mother is buried, borders and thresholds are crossed, a son is born, Alaska melts, life is given and taken, throbbing. In all this activity, moments of attention and blessing shine out, crossing over into words where they are, briefly, held.

Margaret Gibson
author of *Not Hearing the Wood Thrush* and
Connecticut Poet Laureate

These fine poems work two ways at once. There is the poem on the page, but also signaled is the contemplation that precedes the poem. My sense is the contemplative mode—never easy or settled—prepares the way for the poem. This is a book of faith, a faith that has wriggled its way to life in the world.

Maurice Manning
author of *Railsplitter*

Only someone looking for truth could reveal its brilliant appearance: "as out of a snow squall, / into a star-shot night." These are emblematic poems, imagistic unities, with form and content in harmony, helping us to see how earth and heaven come together when "The green mother opens her arms to all of us . . ." "Checkpoint," typical of the best in this collection, reminds us that all we may wish to declare, though inadequate for the authorities, is all we have for poetry. There is no better heartbreak than a poem that breaks your heart.

Mark Jarman
author of *The Heronry*

Jeffrey Johnson's poems exists in a twilight world of rest and restlessness. They do not shy away from the complexities of a life of faith. They listen to angels, weary of their glory, but they still sing doxologies that praise "all who tried to make it, up and down / Main Street, with dreams that needed more traffic, / of a less familiar kind." Rich, earnest and reverential, these poems pay loving attention to our lives on earth.

Jason Gray
author of *Radiation King*

Jeffrey Johnson's poems draw us into intimate relationship with earthbound life—birth, childhood, parenting, aging and death. In vivid, painterly and euphonious language, they evoke the natural world and the spirit that dwells within and beyond all flesh. Quiet and melancholic, alert and attentive, some of them seem almost like prayers. They will help you notice—come into the presence and feel—the power of life, in all of its ordinariness and splendor. Reading this book can be experienced as a kind of prayer.

Richard Chess
author of *Love Nailed to the Doorpost*

This Will Be a Sign

Poems by Jeffrey L. Johnson

for Lynn + Sue
— Jeff Johnson

Fernwood
PRESS

This Will Be a Sign

©2020 by Jeffrey L. Johnson

Fernwood Press
Newberg, Oregon
www.fernwoodpress.com

Printed in the United States of America

Cover and interior layout and design: Mareesa Fawver Moss

Author photo: Itala Keller (https://www.italakeller.com/)

Cover photo: Redd Angelo

ISBN 978-1-59498-066-4

for Kirsten, Matthew, and Nate

Contents

The sun was growing larger as it slipped down the sky. "You sit here every day?" Joseph asked. "You never miss?"

"I never miss except when the clouds cover. I am the last man to see it."

—John Steinbeck, *To a God Unknown*

Better that we conceive of dawn than noon,
That place where all things shift, and middle night
Sits for its portrait in half light, and still
Sits obstinately in two lights, quite still.

—L. E. Sissman, *Canzone: Aubade*

"Grandfathers, you where the sun goes down, you of the sacred wind where the white giant lives, you where the day comes forth and the morning star, you where lives the power to grow, you of the sky and you of the earth, wings of the air, and four-leggeds of the world...to you I offer this pipe that my people may live!"

—Black Elk

Pentecost

I'll hold you up for a breath of the wind
through cottonwoods chattering, flapping,
at four swallows passing two sawtooth aspen
applauding and cheering cumulus clouds
passing by in parade on an iced sky.

The wind's a gruff elder, at home here.
He'll tickle your face till you laugh,
eyes scrunched, lips curled up in a grin,
or you gasp and cry out when dust caught
in his beard brushes across your bare skin.

The wind's a kind watcher, she whispers
ssshh through conifers in line by the barn.
If you lie here, on a blanket, under the windmill,
you might feel a loved one next to your face,
wishing you well on your ancestors' hill.

Night School

His messengers must have let him know
that soon he will outgrow our arms and our hands.

So when his sleep ebbs, and he rolls into our bed,
we stir and admit in drowsy locutions

that birds have nests, soothed with stray threads
and lined with down from their own breasts,

and foxes have dens where the soil is cool
as the first fall and feel of the pillow.

His heart breaks next to ours in unspoken
awareness that sooner or later we all sleep alone.

Vacation

This borrowed lake, still as a bored counselor,
barely returns reactions to my tone and twitches.

Green minnows of mind rest in grooves of sand.
Opaque tails flutter, lips pop leisurely,
gills wave like red-threaded dragon wings.

Simple thoughts are small fish at rest before
they trail off like a train of bubbles rising in air.

Summer News

I saw Satan fall like lightning
on a pocked and twisting rooster.

The evening sky was bruised
and roiled when God came booting,
panting, hunting, pelting corn
with wind and shotgun hail.

When God aimed at Jesky's barn,
I saw Satan fall like lightning.
Others saw great balls of fire,
rolling red and orange and gold.

Crack and sizzle, down sailed Satan,
through the splintered hay mow,
to a feed trough where he scattered
sparks across the straw, stiff
and ready, like matches in a box.

Nevertheless

On a hill above the interstate highway race,
two men, bare-headed, black and blue in soot
and coveralls, feed a wood fire, the size
of a compact car, with sheddings of winter.

They work slowly, sowing flame through wood
to soil and air, and think of boats on the water,
of women they've known, and of lunch,
not of the method or the end of their work.

The progress of fire through pine warms them.
An old-farmer smoke loafs between them,
pleasing the men as the *paraclete* might:
sarcastic, then silent, hanging with them at home.

Late Autumn

The white of an apple,
turned out into air,
is the thin-place of fall.
Children can taste it
on wind off the lake.
Lawns iced over lively
with winter, refracted
in splinters of silver,
signal refinement
of fruit flesh and seeds
into fire for the firs
and gold for her hair.

Forget Your People

Home is his leather recliner
in front of the television.

He walks in and sees you in it,
sorting foreign dreams,

and even though he does not ask
how long you intend to stay,

in the morning you rise and walk
a blue mile to a place where you

strike a new fire for your own
to meet their ghosts of well-being.

Hostel Americans

They leap the Atlantic
like salmon barging currents
to old spawning pools.

They are free and forgiven,
but they have not heard this,
so they eat dust, sip bottled water

and leave foreign tracks
on cobbles worn smooth
by Europe's old meanness

until they slump home to bury
their noses in cubicle stations
where visions cool and dry.

August First

Orange juice sun warms maple syrup
and melts inhibitions into brown-sugar sand.

Undressed with our babies, on the lap of Lake Blue,
we sip juices and nap until rain races through.

Then we shower together and leap across floods
to green stoves that hiss for the boil and roast.

After coffee and chocolate, colors melt in the sky
above Blue: orange creme into grape spilling
raspberry swirl into lemon chiffon.

Flashlights and fireflies grin after ten, peeping notes
of noon's bonfire sun between black, needled arms.

This Will Be a Sign

It might have been an aspen
or some other fairer specimen,
not one of the ghoulish leather
hands of oak-fall that wind-whip
a crackling plague every year.

Soft lime and canary, it bore
the bitten beginning of a bruise,
a brownish canker of dissolution.
I froze, calculating this token
of a mid-autumn afternoon.

With nothing to give in return for
its fruity smoothness, when you
said, here, daddy. I said, thanks,
buddy. I'll see you at three for
the last soccer game of the year.

Eye Fish

Crepuscular rays, the best for my interests, spread
warm and deep for the drag of my lines.

Small fish swim by, and a few big fish float low
like an eagle above or a beast on the floor of the forest.

Fish abound when water rises in colors like this.
Schools of thought advance in thickness of water

folding out satin and silver; eyes turn to it, with
brains sinking into the darkness that swallows

bright flashing baits of liquid eyes stained to match
soil, leaves and sky: earth, emerald and azure.

Better Heartbreaks

Louise wore red cashmere
on New Year's Eve the year her James died.
He laid out a clean suit, put on silk pajamas,
and died under a down comforter.

My mother rode in on the first Greyhound
she could catch to sit with her cousin Louise
and stare down demons peering in
around corners and out from closets.

When our station wagon turned to the city
each season, my mother called ahead
to Louise, and we trouped up for visits with her.

My brothers and I were chips and Coke boys.
Louise served V-8 and fruit.

When her big poodle Jo-Jo turned gray
and died on a pillow overlooking the river,
no other eyes shared the Mississippi with her,
so she moved to the woods and there remarked
gracefully at such as a feather-tailed squirrel.

She doted on strangers at her door,
hummingbirds and newspaper boys.

She sent books on Christmas and birthdays.
Inside gift cards of snow on pale mountains,
or of bamboo shade, was her sign: Love, Louise.

She loved Paris and Vienna, pressed, smiling
days there with her James, Esquire.

She loathed the local cityscape, its heat
on her face, greasy breath and loud alleys.

And rough, rural religion—the bare arms of God—
did not match the flow of her clean mind,
liquid voice, creamy skin.

One day an admirer came to her, unannounced,
and kissed her cheek.
Louise let the lech stay, sheltering it new
every morning and evening, sitting patiently
for its thirsty affection.

In the dead of December, police kicked down her door.
Louise was in bed with that guest of three years.

Her body was a wisp of a drift in the Alps,
thin as a runaway wolfhound.

Robed doctors scolded her: Why did you wait?
Nurses, attending her, thought they were at tea.

The night of her death, she would not hold a hand.
When deep breathing began—that lover,
all through her again—

Louise asked, what's going on here?
What is going on here now?

Float Nights

Some summer evenings we piled in
for a ride to A & W Root Beer stand.

If it was not a float night, we would settle
for ice cream cones or cold mugs of root beer.

If we had parked facing west, we could have
watched sunsets through poplars, over soy beans.

We never learned how he decided on float nights,
when a carhop would balance a towering tray.

The sun may have been setting like sorrow
behind us, but ice cream was rising in root beer.

Black Leather and Horse Flesh

Five days before Christmas. No snow,
but the old-fashioned wind was on time.

She swept down Main Street as she did
in the days of black leather and horse flesh,
when she thought she owned the place.

Under the spray of the Milky Way stars,
a boy pedaled away with an elephant,
wrapped as a present, for his new brother.

A baby mouthed a pink elephant's ear
when the wind finally seduced the new snow
and, in regal authority, to a town draped

in garland and decked out in sparkles,
decreed it a jewel. The kingdom had come.

Advice

Children, don't quit the piano.
Sit through scales and arpeggios.
Wade through pieces assigned to you.

Don't quit without earning suppleness
enough to filter music
from the page to your fingers.

If you quit too soon, on some middle-aged
evening, your lead fingers will land
between the white and black keys,

and your own children will lay on
paternal hands, and say, we didn't know
you took lessons. How many years?

Done with the Compass and Chart

Wild nights! Wild nights!
Were I with thee,
Wild nights should be luxury!

—Emily Dickinson

How could we find our way into your
old-man dreams when your restless nights
blended with morning naps in seamless
recliner twilights, washed in the grace
of cable sports that turned every midweek
morning into Sunday afternoon?

Your wild nights, charged with signals
behind heavy eyelids, were blurs
of turnpikes in the rain, drag races
on abandoned runways, floods around
boarding gates, lantern swarms and horns
of stations, swirls of shifting stars.

I would have gone with you, sat behind
you, bending my ear to the thin sound
of the radio, on one of our races across
the manic-depressed prairie to the lap
of your mansion, with its thermostat
adjusted to cool or warm our dreams.

Some Sacrifice

The birds pick and choose along buffet corn rows.
The cocks spread their iridescence to the red sun.

A priest's acolyte appears to pursue those sun-princes
behind capes and curtains of scalloped corn leaves.

In the pop of an instant, in the fulness of time,
the world stops, and the acolyte completes her service.

Crazy Horse

Europeans rode west on rails.
Their dreams never turned back
as they turned for the Sioux:

to the sun going down and around,
like a wheel in a wheel, to a hunt
and a rolling move, dark out of dusk,

to the moon and a dance coming
'round to the sun again, and off
to a raid for fresh horses.

White folks kept a lineage of names
half-remembered, drawn of air, not
from the earth, names like Sitting Bull,
Red Cloud, Spotted Tail.

The boy's father, Crazy Horse, named
his son Curly, until the day the boy
rode out nearly naked for a fight
and was not harmed by two lions.

Then the father gave the boy
his name—Crazy Horse—and an average-
size, light-skinned legend was born,

a human weapon with a heart for the poor,
who rode sunsets to ledges
wide enough for a thin man's night's rest.

The Plague

Hundreds of starlings descend on my yard,
taking over the trees in refugee fellowship.

Juiced by the season, they jaw their opinions
and call out themselves in bird-sound
so thick they can ride it together on a plan
long implanted within and among them.

The wind in the trees has a word of its own
for the birds and for me: all flesh is grass.

So, immigrant-style, the black birds flock
and fly off before winter (today, just a shiver)
arrives, landing hard with both feet.

I call out to my own: Who needs me today?
Who's leaving today? Who's leaving today?

Crepusculum

Sore from serving,
a mother held her daycare baby
in the belly of a bus.

She hushed it hard with softness
until the cries muffled down
under the engine and the tires.

She turned her face into the hood
of her sweatshirt and flew
from there, eyes-closed and free.

Other riders reached over to her.
Let your baby breathe, child;
a baby's got to breathe, you know.

Against a gray sky, shamed
and abandoned again, birds
arranged themselves as silhouettes.

Getting by on crumbs of the day,
landed birds rested and tucked
their heads under their wings.

Sense of Direction

He knew the way to crossroads towns.
He could roar to locations he thought of
on the lake, beyond land-sight,
where I was at sea without his direction.

Why that sense was not given to me,
when it was given even to unimpressive
dogs that do not fret fences in their way,
or come when called, I do not know.

Exercises

Up early for cartoons, I would walk past
my father, in a strap T-shirt and boxer
shorts, into his old navy calisthenics.

Later, toes on the line with my gym class,
I followed Gizzy's round of exercises that
worked every muscle in the human body.

After the drills, Giz rolled out the season's
balls for us to use on our own, freeing
him to fold towels and nip on gin he hid.

Fever

I imagine my boys, grown up
from kids, with erratic plans,
to still men, in place under the sun,
their days numbered against the sum
of history's tombs and mountains
of bones, murmuring dry complaints.

They stopped for a moment, but did not
answer when I asked how they weigh
their lives against their fate of days.

I prayed they would not have answered
that they shiver no changes of weather
off their skin, never wish for home fires,
never swim in strange desires, never slur
a sea chant or scan an ancient tale
for help in battle or in pursuit of love.

A Natural History

In those days a young woman
braided green blades, felt quahogs
in the silt with her toes, and gave shells
to the river, which flushed them,
with thanks, to the tide, allowing the sun
rest ahead of its palsied rising.

Broken in already, that girl stood in smoke
and sang when she saw the moon,
with the sun rising below it, and an otter,
slick and black as the boy she laid with
the night before, dance with a herring,
like starlight, in its mouth.

Moons later, outside another young woman's
window, snow scrubbed the metal-tooth tangle
of hardtop and steel that had grown up
where breath used to rise warm over soft,
brown banks of the Hudson.

She sang as she forked tuna onto greens
and looked out on snow falling frantically,
as if to persuade her not to draw shade
but to sing back the peace of the place.

All Aboard

The night train's idling and ready
to rackle over rickety tracks,
through grown-over green.

This train's always on time, click-
clacking with a band playing blue
glitter notes until the first a clerk,
taking tickets, appears as the first ray.

Cockadoo! Howdyadoo everyone!
Doors yawn open, glistening and wet
from the moist maw of night.

Long Live the Weeds

What would the world be, once bereft
Of wet and of wildness? Let them be left,
O let them be left, wildness and wet;
Long live the weeds and the wildness yet.

—G. M. Hopkins, from "Inversnaid"

Thorns and burs it will offer.
Life in the weeds is bearded and bent,
green, bleeding, persistent.

Gathered and graceful,
life in the weeds is hand-me-down;
stalks reach into your pocket,
runners stream around your ankles.

Life in the weeds winds down
and presents small white blossoms
along the ground, and traces up
skinny-as-cowboy trees.

Life in the weeds smells of stones
and sand on the edges of worked-up soil.
Life in the weeds lies beyond procedures
and between measurements.

Life in the weeds is for strays and
for bums, for hunters, and for children
who won't come when called
from the dew-grabbing edge of evening.

Life in the weeds holds an old hope
for a wilderness garden to spread,
before plans laid out on blue paper
are stamped and approved.

Crepusculum II

Three Dakotas kneel next to their horses.
Wide-brimmed hats shade their eyes,
black braided hair falls down their backs.

They turn away to the setting sun
when they feel eyes fall on them, and sense
that a warning or a greeting might follow.

A breeze picks up grass to brush the horses
and dust the Dakotas' cowboy clothes.

Wrapped to themselves, they stand,
spread darkness over their horses, and walk
off to the west, into someone else's dream.

Burial of the Gravedigger's Mother

This grief to him was like standing in sand
up to his knees, and water up to his chin.
His sister's grief swelled and receded;
she bobbed and leaned on her daughter.

In a suit for the first time since he laid
his father's bones there, and his forearms
ached to the weight of the casket,
he stepped forward with his family to pray.

Another day he would have snapped quiet
orders to focus his boys and steady their arms
for placing the solemn crate in front of
trembling hands and swaying bodies.

Today he stood still for the Amen before
slipping away from the black net of respect
to his huddle of canvas coats schooled
together with an old elm that steadied him.

He tapped out an unfiltered Camel, lit and
cupped it as if it were a dear thing, let the
smoke gather and lift off to lighten his mood
on that strange aquamarine of a day.

Morning in the Circus Camp

The elephant trainer wakes before dawn.
He lights a Marlboro and presses his hand
to his three sacred mountains, all belly
and butt in a line under night lights.
He dozes on a cot, the color of his beasts,
in a corner, before the whole camp stirs.

One Chinese tumbler is up making tea
after dreaming all night of American girls.
He wonders what morning would be after
dancing till two with a blonde from Chicago,
and what the five others would say if he
screeched in by cab for the morning rehearsal.

Angela draws shade against the new sun
but keeps a draft open, because this is her time
to fly with the red and blue birds as she did
near the river, when she was a child.
Then, with delts and glutes pumping famously,
Angela and her partner, Francesco, make love.

The old clown needs only five hours of sleep.
He's up sweeping his trailer and grieving
his Esther who died in their doublewide
outside of Phoenix. She was bald as his
headpiece, and made up with rouge
and shadows to set off her fathom-less eyes.

The dog lady gives in to a menthol smoke
before brushing the coffee-brown back
of Brutus, a Great Dane, on his cinnamon futon.
Dachshunds and schnauzers awakened from
drawer space under her bed, scratch and slide
over paisley linoleum and pile at the door.

The horse trainer lies still, drawing strength
from the grace and power of her animals.
Divorced, she thinks of her three scattered
children, but not of him, asleep, with his hand
on a breast of the woman who walks a high
wire, juggling weapons and batons of fire.

Evening Prayer

We've almost forgotten
to sing the sun down:

in candle-lit vespers,
where cowled troops turn out
to sing *phos hilaron*,
serious and steady;

at an evening sacrifice,
near the edge of the world,
where the sea fingers in
along the tired shore;

in a grotto, off a side street,
where a deacon serves
amber confessionals
and gold penitentials;

out in a clearing,
where a campfire holds orbits,

or here at this table,
limbs folded, eyes pillowed.

Ignored in the evening,
the sun may rise dog-faced,
meat teeth lacerating the flesh
of our labor, indoors and out.

Put to bed with a song,
the sun might return
like the palm of a hand, running
rays through the waves of the wind,

soothing the backs of old fields,
jostling new feathery growth
that turns up like a fuzz
on the side of a hill.

Sighting

A tattered old soaker finally shuffles off
to oblivion in the impassive lap of the Atlantic.

Three finches in the locust are brushed by shade
from frayed linings of the storm's coattails.

Illumined in movement, the birds are lemon
ornaments, set in dripping, adolescent foliage.

They blink and twinkle like last night's lanterns,
above a brace of mallards dabbling in the puddles.

Alaska Is Melting

The beast of a bandit,
who rides the night sky,
glares into a hole in our tent.

The camel wilts the edges
of Fairbanks and softens
the streets of Nome.

Caribou feel aged
by three years of antler weight;
their cloven steps
dent the tundra in January.

Missile-packed salmon,
red-faced and burly,
turn snouts downward,
raking pearly bellies
over the grit and green bottom
of a creamy emerald river.

The eagle glares sideways
and rises to call ca-aack!
Why wasn't I warned?

Two Ways to Fly

There's flying in a dream
over half-familiar landscapes,
such as old industrial cities,

where affection steams, passion
and boredom punctuate ambition,
loneliness piles like steel shavings.

Then there's dying: a short flight
across farmland symphonies
to evenings of my first flights.

Last Supper

In a lake town whiter than snow,
a father presided, calling out fun
the family had, to which others
added amendments or amens.

Startled by his loud encouragement—
Oh yeah! Order strawberry pie!
I was mistaken for a monitor.

I only wanted to join their swaying
through dessert, the evening before
they drove south where snow is rare,

and children laugh, and moms call
y'all better put on coats and caps
like the quiet folks up north wear.

Winter Break Blessing

I wish our young server could find sun
for her skin, while it's smooth, and for
her hair, while it falls down her back

in walnut and blackberry honey, that
she could feel a bite of salt on her legs,
and ocean fingers begging her ankles,

that she could hear sun-bleached words
until five, then find a buzzed evening
away from the ocean's pawing advances.

Entertainment Tonight

A solstice is a turn on the oval track.
Stars stretched on blue night marvel
at orbs racing round, spinning back.

Then comes a flock of red and orange
fowl, marching along the Milky Way.

They crow cock-a-do to the solstice.
I put on my jacket. The wild-eyed
birds disturb the pock-faced moon.

One evening

without bit or lead you came after me,
over a bent-grass path, to bring me home.
You knew that I could hold out a long time,
all day and night, in the farthest corner of the field,
as I had proven I could, many times before.

Doxology

Praise worn tires rooster tailing dust,
television news in the evening, black coffee,
rhubarb pie in the afternoon before the sun
goes down like a country song, and bunches
of lights ripen around the softball field.

Praise the young ones roaring out of town,
racing past the city limits sign.
When the beer runs out, gravity pulls them
in through an inky prairie night, across
the grease slick outside Case Implements.

Praise physical exams for the football players
before they straggle out at dawn onto wet grass,
groaning like cattle who have gotten sour feed,
moaning like a herd in line across the valley.

Praise all who failed on Main, with dreams
that needed more, and less familiar, traffic.

Anniversary

Under a shelter of shame—a willow,
growing above me in a compost
of too many years away—I wept
the short day out and tried to adjust
to a long day dawning without him.

He worked hard against the dust
his body was becoming, gulping air
in rhythm to settle it.

I gasped beside him, matching my
breath with his, as if his contained
spirit I could translate into stammers
for my own boys, so that the language
of fatherhood would not die with him.

Exit Interview

Did those days pass slowly, as
mine did for me, weeding soybeans,
fishing for carp with canned corn
in the Cottonwood, baking on
the WPI cement pool deck,
ducking tornadoes, waiting out
January blizzards then stepping
out onto squeaking snow?

Or did they pass quickly, as it seemed
to me yours did, here where
roads are mapped and plowed,
steps are measured out, every blade
trimmed to keep your class safe,
with adults on guard against idleness
and unplanned schedule breaks
that might lead to a daydream.

Come With Me

Are your afternoon naps
like fishing on opening day?
Are your naps like casting
in mist-becoming-rain
to a bite that runs you deep?

Covered by the sports pages,
in the neither-here-nor-there,
do you hook your childhood?
Do you taste your mother's jam,
or face your father motoring out
for walleyes with you?

Seek My Face

Children of earth, wherever your bodies rest,
direct your selves out with the breathing tide.

Have no anxiety for the far shore before you,
no regret for the near shore behind you.

Peer down for the deep, living darkness below;
look up high for the darkness beyond the stars.

Bob in fear and love beyond the toll of bells.
Seek my face on the earth's wild water.

Blow out on a current in the spirit of the Galilean
who handpicked water men from an arid land.

The sea is love, and this is truth: the word spread
deep, as the volume of the body, and the eye of love.

Reprise

O gentle, good death, Francis and the monks
knew where you lived and what you smelled like,
and how it felt to touch you and sit with you
in the bloom of their lives.

That was their burden and their blessing.

The tomb in the garden is silent and empty now,
and all that remains on Zion, and in the arks
and sanctuaries, are whiffs twisting toward Jordan,
to the Salt Sea, and out to the Mediterranean.

The green mother opens her arms to all of us.
So come, Lord Jesus, lead us home to her,
your stepmother, in whom you rested peaceful
and still, free of the ages and the aches thereof.

Nicodemus

Nicodemus was out with the cats
in the slack black mouth of Jerusalem.

The city was damp with the day she had eaten
still thick as a film on the walls of her mouth.

Grooming himself, he tasted the darkness
and questioned the breath that seemed like shelter.

Murmurs returned, beating, beating: no one could
see, no one could enter, no one had ascended.

Nicodemus drew his knees to his heart and tried,
without cover, to ride out the night, until

a dew-eyed donkey, bent to his master's bread
cart, pulled in the sun from beyond the Jordan.

Hoop Dancing

Proposing hoop dancing, without broadcast
or scoring, on a stage set for kids starved
in their hearts for battle as much as for art.

Tacky parquet, a caramelized treat, is ready
for the hungry young feet of a traveling troupe,
the fresh, and now famous, Hoop Dancers.

A boom box explodes, and a small bag of bones
bounces onto the stage; beating, drumming,
dribbling pepper-and-pop, he loops and jumps.

In the background, black arms sway, circling,
dunking, dancing fundamentals for an hour
and a half, lighting up night in the city.

Program

Two Russian women in black
play Hungarian Dances for Four Hands.
They bob and twist, digging out nodules
from the crumble of time, without caring
or noticing that it's snowing outside.

Back in Russia, winter's convenient.
Lives slide smoothly along the ice and freeze.
Hands and reinforced wrists turn up a harvest
of roots from white fields, to feed us,
the few who came, hungry for Brahms.

Without

A poet without a god to deny
is like a kiss without a squeeze,
like a lover without a lie,
like coffee without caffeine,
apple pie without ice cream.

A poet without a working
relationship with a god is like
a dealer in empty boxes,
like a shell gamer in the rain,
like a cab driver new to town.

A poet without one good god
on speed dial is like a dog
without a bone, like a rooster
without a cock-a-doodle at dawn,
like a trout without a pool
curling light around its fins,
making time stand still.

A poet without a prayer
is like a song without a singer,
like fineness without feeling,
like beauty noticed without
distance for a backward glance.

A poet not on a first-name basis
with a god holds up the line,
gums up the works, invades
personal space, spoils the soup,
spills hazardous waste across
the highway, is a coward in the ring
and a menace behind the wheel.

Last Night's Lament

When enemies camped around me,
even at the door of my room,
he appeared with a gang
of eleven and twelve-year-olds,
flipping skateboards and spitting seeds.

Before I could tell my grandfather
to grow up, he skid his board
down a handrail and over a trash can
to face up with me
and offer his youth in my defense.

Deck Party Dream

This is my dad, for those who don't know.
You can see, he's a very young man,
far younger than I am.

He's thin and cool.
He wears flowered shirts.
His wrap-around shades are the kind
young men wear on the beach.

Hi Dad! What's the rush?
I could go out with you and your friends.
Not a chance? Okay, but someday
I'll wear those rims and those fancy pants.

Easter Morning

Vested clergy, their souls engorged
by millennia of annual hunts
for an elusive Lord Christ, lead shuffles
of caffeinated seekers across parking lots.
Their parades track alleluias
and scatter astonishments over chilled
pavement and past sheds, still mum
from the night before.

Their processions spread praises
near dumfounded dumpsters below
crane-neck lights blinking and dozing.
Softened by therapy of the sun, soil
beside the asphalt waits for seeds
to be pressed in, and for root-ball offerings
to be presented from the knees,
to the altar of the earth, prepared today,
as on no other, for growth of mystery.

Now I Lay Me Down

Our moldable armful,
new lumps of baby boy,
bumping my shoulder
and missing his mother
with calf moan and kit call,
is sharp-joint wolf-pup
flesh, alive on the bed.

Arms punch and legs spring
from puddle to picnic ground,
sandbox to garbage can.

Don't hug me!
Lift me high to the ceiling!
Drop me hard on the bed!
What am I now? A bag of oats?
Spill me over the covers!

Back arched, he kicks off sleep,
his sneakers, his brown bear,
and my fumbling hold
on the flubbering first
sweet-breath years of his life.

Does Jesus bite fingers?
If Jesus were here
I would ask him to thumb wrestle.
Bring in my dump truck please!
Don't close the door,
and don't leave me!

Beneath blue bathing eyes,
his chin snaps to end the romp.

Tell Mom to check me.
Maybe she knows
where the stairway to heaven is.
Bring me a glass of water.
Now I lay me down.

Black Wool Days

I would pick him up, and he would sit in,
smelling of lanolin, a man without an umbrella
to his name, but with two suits of raingear
the color of the lake under storm clouds.

He would see that his grandsons are fine.
The two of them might remind him of himself
and his brother Joe, who knew at least
that fishing is the study of silence.

He might start to notice tangled lines
in my mind, and would look straight ahead,
turning over the thought that his son's son
had become a stranger to him.

He would not comment, but he would not see
much improvement from leaving behind
what he knew: weather-talk, flat land, walleyes,
neighbors close but not too close.

My boys would stare at his long nose,
smell *Luden* cough drops on his breath,
Bay Rum on the thin skin of his neck,
and touch the wool fedora on his head.

Along the way, he would show me
what I thought I knew and remembered,
and I would tell him things that had no hold
in his heart and no corner in his mind.

In his black-wool childhood, he learned
not to care for ethnicity romanticized,
or poverty lionized, in a self-directed,
American forward march.

That's why I stopped for him: to ask if he knew
where he is in me today. I might ask him,
what is truth? Because I know that truth is not
what I write about him, and not what I remember

and not what I think I know about his life.
Truth is a borderland of murky scenery
and poor visibility that we drive out of,
as out of a snow squall, into a star-shot night.

Late Feeding

A fair wind blows in two ways:
from a pug nose and a bud of a mouth.

This breath was not felt twelve days ago,
when black bathed and pillowed the head.

Now currents crackle curves on his scalp,
thundering tympanum, rumbling out charges

over flushed, powdered skin, ruffling roots
of feathery hair, green wheat in the wind.

Prelude

Elohim snort and pace over the face
of nothing, sobbing oceans, blowing tides
and breakers into hysterical rolls
and roaring miles of spray and foam.

They bellow and huff, red-eyed and urgent,
big bulls aching for flesh, and wild for blood.
Over that brine of lonely tears, Elohim set lights,
two courting gifts to shine on their dream stage.

With the recovering sea reflecting their faces,
they offer their fantasies, one by one.
In a circle, by turns, images in the minds
of overheated Elohim appear in earth tones
and potential, and are declared good.

Sanctus

Holy holy holy day without a dawn,
we, the six-winged seraphim,
are weary of glory going on and on.

Lord, lay down upon an eon!
Cool off this eternal flame house.
Simmer, steam and rest.

We intoned that, did our best, but
without a hint of dimming for relief.

So, we, with the Almighty,
remain eyes-in-burning-eye. Amen.

Wings of cherubs brush our faces
with their insulated feathers,
stirring stars and spinning wheels
around the throne in endless noon.

High and holy evermore!
Light has won, daylight is heaven,
and we are on, past the fizzling sun.

Night Fishing

Shoeless on the sand, he lashes frayed nets
and pinches kelp from knots of skein,
brown as his blood-brother's hands.

His own overdone skin is dusted with silt
when water welcomes his boat's greenish glide.

The water caresses and slaps his boat's bottom
until passion raises waves of size-heaving-size.

Elusive fish swim in granular soup.
Unsleeping, they feed in black billows, nervous
in currents of water as smoke is in dry air.

Drawn to weak rays like first light, sweet catfish
and carp come to settle their lives near a
light shining in welcome through midnight.

A Voice in Ramah

Sleep piles and drains
through the crannies and fissures
of frozen black hours.

Time slowed to slug thoughts
and lead steps toward coffee
is ticking behind doors ajar.

In the half-light of those rooms,
fear is a face with wide eyes
at the side of the bed.

One floor below them,
agony rains an emergency.
Life twists toward the light.

In the monitors' moan, darkness
presses in, and a seedling lies still
in the arms of an angel.

Peace falls leaden and velvet when
she whispers, meet me at the shore.
We'll go home from there.

Agnus Dei

By late afternoon, even the dark side
of the earth had lost the sun's light.

Fires spit grease sparks, and our virtues
lay frozen in a dry blackened sun.

When morning broke again over Eden,
the *mysterium tremendum* resembled
a relative's brow, intent on his compost.

Good morning, brother! Growing roses
and corn from that confidence under your feet?

Salvation, spaded with that confidence,
appeared in green nip and red bud.

A blade rose thin through the thaw, and
radiance returned to ride high, like a prince,

on a marching ray of the first working day.

ICU

What more do they want
with their wires and flashes?

Why don't they ask directly
what she did with the cash
and whether she loved
the friend she kept for pleasure.

She will not say a word
until morning dawns as a man
dressed in white
with a rinse for her brow.

Cool cotton pressed between
his flesh and her flesh
weeps wishes from the sweet
well of her youthful years.

Only then does she break open
a story of love, and admit secrets
she kept folded and hidden.

Now and Forever

Our father in heaven tucks into himself
at the top of his dive.

He arches his back to match the span
of the black dome above his body.

Hallowed be his name, echoing in tumbles
all the way down to his landing.

Our daily bread received, the counter
rubbed down, no cumulus rain-maker

rinses through to drive us to sadness
before the star of morning arises in the east.

Taste and See

A tired spotlight cuts
a rough tunnel through
weeknight darkness
to a basement classroom
brightened like a blessing
for them to try, taste
and swirl served notes,
their voices climbing,
tumbling, following, chasing,
repeating, completing runs
through eternal fields
of Mendelssohn and Bach.
Sound leaps and dances
from diaphragm stages,
through bellows of lungs,
to evolved, vibrating skulls.
The taste is salt lick, grain
snap, and a bouquet of wine:
music as a banquet, spread
and served by the choir.

Hope This Helps

Unclothed and wilted on cotton
that last night was crisp,
we lay awake in half-dreams
of sixty-five degrees
when a bare breeze addresses us
and inspires me to find a fan,
and let it blow high
with cooling from Labrador,
and low across the bed
with wind from Lapland,
where red-cheeked children play
in snowflake sweaters
and skate until late on blue ice.

Time Please

At twilight you try to hold yourself
and the frayed day together.

You gather your strength,
but the day can't hold on,

because tomorrow, that bastard,
has it by the hair, and all your sure

pleasure has flown with the sun
to a black hole where a new day

is baked and sent here, dew-wet
and unwanted.

A bloody spilled sunset is all
that remains of the old day.

You don't mention how much
it meant to you, because, after all,

you have a big house, plenty of room,
and unlimited TV in the corner.

Do Not Be Afraid

If you can focus your eyes
on that bird on the bench,
the one in the charcoal suit
with the off-white shirt,
see that it's a proper bird,
with a formal tail tipping,
and its head swiveling socially.
Notice how it flaps straight up
and lands on the same spot,
with a bug on its breath.

See it there on the bench, not
as a specimen, example, kind
or type, not as a pet to be held,
not as a carcass for the market,
or as a sacrifice for the altar,
but as a small bird on a bench.
Then you will have prayed,
and prayed well, I would say,
as if you loved an ordinary
and otherwise unnoticed bird.

Mercies

Incense, rising, sliding, reneging
like a forked and fingered snake-
whispered sin, his cigar smoke
scrubbed a cursive communique
in the living room, twisting and
sealing its own inside out, sending
itself to every room in the house.

Out from floods flushing evening
communion, she shot a mist
of air freshener at the spirit of
fried fish, chased out the last of our
liver and onions so that, by bed time,
darkness could pour in from the kettle
of night, to rooms white as porcelain.

Crossing

Ninety-five years old,
she corrected the young man who told
that life was too short for worrying.

Life's not too short, she said.
Life's too long.

She had prayed that before she saw
one more season of flowers down,
brown and wrinkled,
that she would have flown,
like a grackle from the crown of a larch,
one flier alone in a September flock.

But she woke to the first snow
and rolled over to face a white wall.

She had returned thanks for tank cars of tea
and for truckloads of toast,
but now mornings broke full already,
and hours rolled slowly
like freight cars at a crossing.

When the long vagrant train of her days
finally steamed and braked,
she grabbed the handrails with both hands
and hopped off.

Breath of Fresh Air

Out tonight without a jacket,
it's too cool for a walk and too warm
not to signal spring.

That party boy, the holy ghost,
has births and anniversaries covered,
but the bereaved are on their own.

The old body is no longer safely
at home, shuffling through
familiar rooms, from television chair
to refrigerator, and to bed after sports.

Tonight the air declares the spirit's curse:
from now on every expedition
will be an alien exploration, every mild

new venture, a high wire act, without
the imaginary net he held below.

I Thirst

His face was locked in a bronze mask.
His body was imprisoned in sand like cement.
A gull, its feathers on fire, its eyes hungry
for sin, landed like a law in front of him.

Then a company charged, scattering sparks,
sweeping clouds with blood-red streamers,
splitting waves with sharp-toned brass,
leveraging the brightest stars to lift him.

Checkpoint

A border guard asks:
anything to declare?
I feel I must admit
that I'm carrying
part of my grandfather's pain.

He studies my face
and flips through regulations.
I continue, coming clean:
I am weighed down
with my father's regret.

He looks over his glasses at me:
Any rare fauna or exotic plant
life in your possession today?

Of course not, I say.
My father was an oak tree,
not an exotic.
Isn't your father an oak too?

Did strangers approach you
to carry things over?
No? Stand aside anyway,
so those with nothing to declare
may pass on ahead of you.

First Night

His first night fell as he rested
from planting a lemon tree in his yard.
It had been a good long day,
growing up on a farm of white buildings
with a pair of Belgians.

One spring day he fell through river ice,
and that one time was waited on and
warmed by a bath and popcorn.

In the city, where he never wanted to be,
he earned a degree and a title, found
a woman who liked to dress up and dance
with him through Arizona winters
that chilled off like pleasure.

Awakened in remembrance, he might tell
of Christmases, of coffee, of the drop-top
red Cadillac he dreamed of but never owned,
of the beagle he named Boy.

He might not tell these things, of course,
if, like a single abstract, all things
are framed and forgotten.

Late Sports News

His thick jowls have fallen;
he wears rimless eyeglasses.
Fifty-three years past his birth
as George Herman, the Sultan
of Swat has throat cancer.

Still, he waits by the phone
in a paisley bath robe
for a long-distance call
from an owner, who promised.

The Babe never managed.
He wants to try that now: mold
an expansion club *ex nihilo,*
make it a team for the ages.

Made in America

The old poets knew that
a jazz-singing father,
coming home over a threshold
of years, renewed the world
for his children.

His singing popped new
constellations in the crowded
winter sky and surprised the ear
with notes above
the melody's highway.

Bending back home,
the father resolved the day,
running refrains
past evening eyes,
composing new verses

behind and ahead
of familiar patterns, until
the sun pulled words and music
out together for another day
of improvisation.

Stopover Town

Can there be another place as lonely
as someone else's small town at sundown?

Discouraging words are all your heart will hear
from gray-washed streets and storefronts.

You won't feel village serenity unless you doze
in a black-and-white rerun in your hotel room.

The town will not share its silence with you,
and its stillness will haunt your stranger's heart.

Shirt and Tie

Your soul sprang from the bed
and released without footfall,

leaving me and a beige chair
exposed as soiled and ordinary.

When you flew from the only life
you knew, the atmosphere turned

over. Clean breaths flushed
my lungs but blew in doubts that

I had given sufficient thought to
proper clothes and shoes for you.

Some of these poems have appeared in earlier versions in *The Christian Century, Christianity and Literature, Journal of the American Medical Association, Kindred, Willow's Wept,* and other journals and webpages. "Do Not Be Afraid," in a slightly different version, won the 2008 Merton Prize for poems of the sacred and has been reprinted in Unitarian Universalist and Moravian publications.

First Line Index

9 781594 980664